BIRDSONG AND FLAME

(A Turkish Diary)

by

James Andrew

Kite Modern Poetry Series

Book Ref : K.T. 136

ISBN 0 907759 20 3

Kite Modern Poetry Series

Series Editor : Kevin Troop

Acknowledgements

Sincere thanks are offered to the editors of the
following, where some of these poems first appeared:
*Envoi; Iota; Lamport Court; New Hope International;
Northwords; Poetry Nottingham International; Poetry
Scotland; The Journal; Understanding;* and *Weyfarers*;

but, in particular, to *Northwords,*
for their constant encouragement.

Thanks also to friends,
family and colleagues at school.

Thanks to Turkey for the inspiration.

To Jennifer,
with thanks for
her patience while
I scribbled away.

Published by
K.T. Publications,
16, Fane Close,
Stamford,
Lincolnshire,
PE9 1HG,
England.

Printed and bound by
MPG Biddles, Ltd.,
24, Rollesby Road,
Hardwick Industrial Estate,
King's Lynn,
Norfolk,
PE30 4LS,
England.

CONTENTS

11   Arrival, Istanbul

13   Morning Walk (Feast Of The Sacrifice)

15   Istanbul Miniatures

17   Rich

19   Part Of The Tour

20   Birdsong And Flame

22   Saturday Alien

24   Istanbul Sound

26   Losing It

27   Ferry Trip

29   Pitched Battle

31   This Time

32   Waiting For The Tremor

33   The Sixth Earthquake

34   For The Moment

36   Bosphorous Bridge

37   Apphrodite

38   Taksim Meydan, Day Of The Match

39   Promenade

41   Dance, Dance, Dance

42   Flower-Seller

43   Istiklal Caddesi

44   Bosphorous

45   Istanbul

47   Metropolis

48   Toothache, Cappadocia

49	Underground City, Derinkyu, Cappadocia
51	Ihlara Canyon, Cappadocia
52	Building Block, High School, Istanbul
53	Afternoon Off
54	Suicide
55	The Disquiet
57	Mothering
59	Looking Through Yesterday's Trouser Pockets
60	Hilal (The Fever After The Operation)
61	Hilal (Recovering)
62	Here Again
63	Coming Out On The Plane Soon
65	Now That You've Gone Away Again
66	New Horizons, Antalya
67	Odd Angle, Antalya
68	The View From The Restaurant, Antalya
70	Free-Wheel, Antalya
71	Cat-Time, Antalya
72	Rainy Day, Antalya
73	Amphitheatre, Ephesus
80	Postcards
81	Return
83	Highland Loch
84	Cattle On Balnakeil Beach
86	Café Moments, Stromness
88	Ruckus, Balnakeil, Sutherland

BIRDSONG AND FLAME

Arrival, Istanbul

I imagine I shake like a pneumatic drill
Shuddering my questions into the night,
As I stand beside my two suitcases
By a Turk I do not know
With his dark eyes and possibly dark thoughts.

Other airport arrivals spill about laughing,
Or speak to each other with guitars.
I solemnly wait to be led
Into darkest midnight Istanbul.
Traffic lurches past,
Its gleam in the airport lights ominous, cold.

Our bus comes.
He pulls me by the arm.
The city opens in the night like a concrete flower,
Its scent carbon monoxide.
I try to leave my fear one pace behind.

Morning Walk

(Feast Of The Sacrifice)

1

Her pink tongue curling and pushing,
As supple as an Olympic gymnast on floor exercises,
The cat was spreading her white fur firmly
Over the black and orange patches on her coat –
Or so it seemed,
Her smile pinned on as tight as a badge.

I walked downtown towards kahvaltı, *
The minutes of my morning lined up
As a row of jams, meats, and breads;
And did my best
To spread my own smugness
Just as tidily.

2

The sheep I passed was lying
Flat on its back with its throat cut.

It was white with rolls of fat
As loose as a padded jacket.

There was no expression on the face
As if it didn't mind,

Or as if it didn't know any more
Whether it minded or not.

It was blood, plentiful,
Like a crowd of people rushing around,

* kahvaltı (Turkish) = breakfast

13

Fat and meat, accidentally
Shaped as a sheep.

A man was wiping his knife clean,
Changing red into silver.

He turned the blade through the air,
A cut of brightness shining in the sun

As he sheathed it in a worn denim bag,
Definitely, like a cat landing on her kill.

3

Announcing our duty
With a swish of her tail against our legs,
The cat triumphed her arrival,
Made herself a procession of rubs
And loiterings for our obeisance,
The nudge of finger against fur
That was long like the flowers
Of a shrub in black bloom,
Limbs as supple as a ballet dancer's,
As she stretched and poised.

We sat in the bahçe in Beşiktaş – *
White plastic tables and tea glasses –
And wondered what cat glissade she would do next
As she twirled for his breakfast –
Hopefully some of our toast.
I slipped her some
As we shared the sunshine
And the Bosphorous, too,

Thrusting its huge self
Tinily against our quay.

* bahçe (Turkish) = garden

Istanbul Miniatures

1

Past this pavement café
They tread their ones and twos,
Slowly pace out a crowd,
Eyes glancing, mouths jammering
In the rhythm of their mid-morning,
Like blood pulsing its steadiness
Through a body.

2

The Bosphorous is the breath of Istanbul.
It sighs in and out,
Sometimes coughing phlegm
In white gasps at the air.

3

These ferries criss-cross
Like white stitches trying
To stitch together a fabric.

4

Cars are like fleas skittering over skin.
I would like to flick off the annoyance
Of their hurry to hurry.
If they could they would
Full throttle through each other,
As they suck the peace
From my morning,
Jump the tarmac and concrete past,
Make the harbour rev off.

5

It is a tall, well-built city,
The muscles of its office blocks strong,
But it gazes out
To a sky that reaches higher
Above buildings, streets, seas:
These limited horizons.

Rich

On the Bosphorous, a white cruiser
Bobs lightness up and down,

As laughter cantatas out
From the casually angled bodies

And the rich raise
Their glasses to today.

Along the shore,
A red Ferrari suaves past,

Signalling something
Optimistic in silver

With the golden
Istanbul sunshine.

The morning treads cheerfully
In tracksuit, Raeboks,

And stereo headphones.
The rich make the pace

As balloon sellers float
Cheap plastic hopes

Cheerfully towards their sun.
Out in the channel,

A powerboat sleeks past
Trailing bubbly behind it

As my eyes struggle to keep up,
And waiters wait, and bus drivers

Drive round in circles
And Istanbul paces up

And down its pavements,
Harassing itself

With traffic and fumes;
And the ordinary lives

Fritter impatiently
At traffic lights

All over the city,
That refuse to signal green.

Part Of The Tour

The push and shove of Turkish voices against you
Threatens you with their wares:
Rip-off watches glitter sunshine and false hopes;
Video CDs glamorise shoddy programming
With pictures of Julia Roberts or Kate Winslet.

Silver rings circle you, poised for the sell,
As you twist them on to straight fingers.
Amber oozes on to stalls, as solid pendants,
Heavy with the promise of a golden pleasure.
Leatherware soft to the touch draws your greed.

Yankee accents drawl wonder and cynicism
Almost at the same time.
Your eyes slip from stall to stall
To a slim Turkish girl angling a bracelet on her arm
And a question towards her boyfriend;

And to a fat Turkish woman trying to tempt you
With pancake and spinach,
As the smell draws in your breath.
A smile from a Turkish face strokes you.
A bargain is yours:

Ortaköy Silver Market, crowds dinning the day,
Stalls a clutter of people and wares
All yours for the moment,
Till your bus draws out and seeks
The next tourist floor show.

Birdsong And Flame

Bird calls skated across from the park,
With the expertise of an Olympic
Performance on ice of *Bolero*,
Executing slick shuffles and extraordinary leaps
Before landing lightly again – as birdsong –
Amidst the strenuous grunts of heaving traffic
And the flat vowelling of gulls.

Out in the Bosphorous, the sun
Tried to turn the water into flame
So that delight torched at us
Out of the sea as well.

And I looked down at the shore
And tried not to see
The plastic bottles and rusting cans,
But to believe instead in birdsong and flame.

Saturday Alien

He wefted himself
Down the Istiklal Caddesi,
Into the furtherness of Istanbul,
Through the tangled weave
Of Turkish words,
Headscarves and sallow skins.

His mind chattered to itself
About their strange custom
Of taking the money to pay for things
From the pockets of other peoples.

A beggar with no legs
Raced after him and pulled at his jacket.

He bought a newspaper written in English.
He needed his own country
Walking round in his head,
To remind himself
That some of the things
He remembered were real.

He felt alien and annoyed that
People kept bumping
Into his red-haired antennae.
His polka-dot fair skin
Was a constant source of amazement.

A child tried to sell him wipes
As tears threatened
To coruscate from his eyes.

When he thought of home
His mind rocketted off.

His body crumpled behind.

23

Istanbul Sound

Sound a pneumatic drill
Splitting the mind
Along with the tarmac.

Even here on Galata Tower
Where I attempt
To overlook everything
The Bosphorous,
Sultanhamet, school,

A ferry siren
Flamethrows its ululations.

A boat bludgeons its diesel
Up the Golden Horn
And into my ears.

The knelling of car horns
Intersects my brain
With tracers of sound.

Someone hammer-grunts
Nails into a roof.

Cars harumph,

Buses grind engines,
As if trying
To wear them down,
Wheeze brakes.

I welcome the silence
Of sun on skin,

Gaze at the quietness
Of clouds drifting

But even here,
Where the mind
Turns in the breeze
And tries to wing
Over the Bosphorous,

Sound megaphones
Istanbul at me.

Istanbul scrapes
The metals of its
Voices in my ears,
Tumults at me unerringly.

Losing It

I tilt forward, feeling
As if I might spill, then jerk back.
The bus dawdles, lurches, stops.

Cars menace against it,
Their exhausts coughing cirrus.

Bodies close in,
A girl's softness passing fleetingly,
A man's rank smell harassing me.

My hand manacles itself to the metal rail.

The darkness of Turks
Weighs on me like a bad memory,
Eyes, hair, looks black.

Outside the bus,
Lights tack past,
Traffic gutters at us.
Darkness looms like a building,
Tall, awesome.

The bus lumbers forward,
Stumbles against the world,
Lights and concrete angles.

It stops, thrusts forward, stops.

I sway into the next moment,
Looking for balance, losing it,
Looking for it again.

Ferry Trip

A tray sways its precariousness,
Teasing our tongues.
Tea glasses flash with
The quickness of laughter
As a waiter urges elma çay on us, * *
His eyes brooding
From one passenger to the next.

The cold slaps my face.
The wind switch-backs my hair.
The scuffed surface of the sea
Turns over its greys,
Greens, and blues.
The ferry judders on
From one part of
The Bosphorous to the next,
From one moment to the next.

A variety of accents
And brightly-coloured
Micro-material jostles me.
Birds nag at our passing.
A dolphin courses off in contempt.

I realise that like the ferry
I too strain through life,
Its spray knocking me
As I pass the cries of strangers
Wondering at me.

* elma (Turkish) = apple

* çay   (Turkish) = tea

The ferry has no patience
With these thoughts
And leaves them behind
As it berths;
And I smell fish
And see a white-jacketed
Restaurateur beckoning at a door,
As he steadfastly ignores
A long-haired black cat.

Pitched Battle

Their long fishing rods
Poke out over the Bosphorous
Like pikes in a mediaeval European battle,
Waiting for the chance
To gore at the enemy cavalry.

Here, these men are attempting
To kill fish: tiny hamsi, *
Gleaming like coins.
They are so small to be pitted
Against such strength,
The technological veracity
Of silver-black carbon-fibre,
So worthless to be matched
Against such buoyant expense.

Their expressionless eyes
Try to take in the whip
Of the enormous poles.
They shimmy up the lines
In dozens, oily anchovies
Ready to be grilled
And soused with lemons.

The gifts of life
Grow smaller but sweeter,
So that men in giant boots
Hurl satisfyingly heavy weights
With all their strength
Towards the far horizon,

* hamsi (Turkish) = anchovies

Stand as an army
Armed with the barb of greed
And the long spear of fate,
Fight their pitched battle

Against such puny scraps of light
That try desperately
To squirm their way back
Into the sweet darkness of the sea.

This Time

The TV news was a disaster movie
About a giant dog who picked up Izmit
And shook it as if it were a rabbit.

We watched as a young girl was carried
Naked out of the rubble.
She was unsure whether to smile,
As if being alive was too much of a surprise to take in.

Several thousand people died or cried a lot.
Camera shots of Turks gripped at your arm
As people complained about broken limbs –
And much worse.
Rescue workers said they felt
They should have had better parts:
They didn't have enough chance to rescue.
Buildings lay about.
Their big scene was over.

None of it seemed real,
As if Hollywood had gone over the top again,
Till the phone rang
And there was a voice from Istanbul I recognized,
Talking about being woken up
By a raving apartment block with the shakes;
And of holding on to his bed
As if it were some kind of mother;
Of the next day, breakfast as normal,
The taste of cherry juice,
Brushing his teeth over an unbroken sink,
Talking to friends who had lost friends and fathers.

The disaster that is always somewhere else
Had knocked just next door,
Had looked him over with no thought
But dismissed him this time.

Waiting For The Tremor

The stars rocketed stillness at us
While we waited to see if the earth

Would shake its fist
As some seismologist had predicted,

But no.
We used words like coins to buy us

A sense of safety,
Talking of known things, like childhood, home.

We'd come from all over,
Canada, America, Australia,

To cower here on a football pitch in Istanbul
In the darkness,

Feeling the fret of grass
And night air on skin,

Looking up to the pell-mell of stars
And the bareness of sky,

Hoping for sameness
In the moments to come.

The Sixth Earthquake

Darkness. Then opening your eyes to more.
The darkness shakes. You shake.

A thin net of light cast into your world of dark
Catches a world uppercutting itself.

Stone walls fidget manically.
A wardrobe tries its hand at moving.

There are sheets you cling on to,
As if afraid they will be heaved off –

A mattress underneath
That seems to be bucking you.

You have become a pneumatic drill
Boring for more light.

Then the world stops
And becomes itself again.

You look at the clock. 3.00 a.m.
You pull up the sheet, turn over.

Nothing to be done
But sleep until day.

For The Moment

The sunlight glances askance
From the Bosphorous
At my dark winter clothes.
A tiny blossom raises itself

Like a pink eyebrow
From the bare black branch of a tree.
Light rubs my tired muscles
Down with the warmth of spring,

Tells me to take on
The bright question mark
Of the day that sees through
Istanbul's pollution

For the first time in months.
The clouds have gone,
Along with the camouflage
Of rain and overcoats.

I am renewed – for the moment,
Skin nudged awake by the sun,
A cotton breeze against it, too,
Soft, cool, as I walk down the coast

Past fishing boats
That dip in and out of the light
That chops its waves
Across the Bosphorous.

Roast chestnuts black with heat
Crack open the kernel of me
With their smell.
The long brown lead

Of a white poodle hunts me.
Balloon sellers not quite
Carried away with it all
Are pulled along the quay

By multi-coloured
'Bouncy castles' on a string.
Spring. A room newly
Decorated with itself.

My eyes open to
The fresh coat of light and air
That gives back
The colours to themselves.

Bosphorous Bridge

That obsessive flittering across the bridge
Of hermit creatures hunched
Into the designer shells that haul them onwards.

What do they protect themselves from?
Just the air that eases up the Bosphorous,
Carrying its salt sharpness like a gift.

I am in a tea garden,
Gazing out over the traffic, and sitting still.
The sun angles down, lunges at the water.

Relentlessly, they carapace across that bridge,
Take the sun's gleam to themselves,
Like a light they are beaming in Morse,

Saying, 'I am here – for now. But follow me.'
They skitter across like slow lightning,
Striking at me, making me
Feel guilty about sipping coffee.

Yet there's nowhere I should be going
On a bridge across the Bosphorous
On a spring day in Istanbul

When the mimosas blaze green,
And the jasmine flames its own yellow message
From its myriad suns.

Apphrodite

(The Archaeological Museum, Istanbul)

Her breasts strike an attitude of innocence
With a knowing boldness.

Here, in the silence, the marble moves
As the sculptor carved it:
In a fold of cloth hanging as if that hip shifted;
The motion of an arm beckoning coyly.

When seeking to express the divine,
The sculptor could only carve a woman
Caught in the surprise of such a perception.

The sculptor carved the goddess of love and beauty
As a small white statue, as if not daring
To make too big a thing out of it,
Just preserve a slight fragility in that angle of nose,
The elegance of that wrist.

I'll never know who it was this sculptor
Used as his model millennia ago,
Yet when she looks at me, her youth taunts me.

Look at that marble smoother than skin,
Those curls caught in the never-ending
Moment of sculpture.

Taksim Meydan, Day Of The Match

A Cimbom red-and-yellow shirt swaggers
A Turk across the square and into me.
Turkey scythes from his eyes
Like a scimitar. I move back.

Galatasaray flags tent down from windows.
Music rocket-launches itself at my ears,
The beat martial, drumming
Testosterone into war-readiness.

The square is a one-sided battleground
Full of Turks machine-gun dancing
In front of speakers and TV screens,
With battle-flags of balloons waving beside them.

The match is an evening away.
Can they frenzy through four hours?
The traffic has been stopped
By barriers. We could walk in peace

If it weren't for this milling mayhem,
This olive-skinned victory over normality at least.
We sneak past, look for a friendly hole.
This is no place not to be Turkish.

There is a football match to be played
For a European trophy.
These Turks are proving something
To the world, whatever it is.

Promenade

Eyes knowing
Their way past you
Along the street;
Black hair strolling,

Short, spiked, flowing,
Posing here, flicking there;
Olive skin frowning,
Perting into

A corner-of-the-lip smile;
Legs rhythming
Blue jeans or flesh tights
Past a beggar,

Crooked limbs
Reflexing into pleas;
Past a covey
Of open wallets

Winging into view;
Milli Piyango lottery
Outnumbering caution;
A gipsy counting fingers

Along her keyboard,
Noting me;
A clockwork toy revolving
Its vendor's selling,

Voice, smile automating
To passers-by
Whose feet pace Saturday
Past the kebabs

Doing their turn;
Past the shirts
In the windows,
Confronting you with

The stares of their
Checks and stripes;
Past gold winking
From the jewellers,

Slyly at your wallet
While the hair struts
And the eyes jerk
Past you unknowingly.

Dance, Dance, Dance

No slack-muscled attempt this,
But a virtuoso, hip-turning,
Thigh-whirling, twist-in-and-out
To the beat of someone else's day

As this loose-skinned man
With fertile, dark, newly-sown chin
Flicks his feet about
Tightly to the rhythm

From the CD and book shop.
Cool guys in denim and shades
Have not half his pace, as they browse
Through CDs and underground magazines,

While the music rockets about, blasting excitement
With the efficacy of semtex.
He has taken a break from his begging
To borrow this day from us weary shoppers.

He tries to catch the rhythm of our leisure,
Force-march his light skip towards our tomorrow
In the clothes of our music,
Clean notes, sharp in the crease of their clarity,

Dance to the crochets of glee –
As we sidle towards the upstairs café,
Lounge in weariness over cappuccino,
Light the measured tread of our cigarettes.

Flower-Seller

Eyes as dark as the coals heaped in his brazier,
A face manacled into the grim business
Of steeling itself against the cold,
He sits huddled into the greased lines

Of his worn, black wool jacket
Beside the tarmac street worn down
By the frantic angling of cars.
Beside him flowers –

The purple and cream of carnations,
The yellow of tulips,
Like drops of colour spilled
From the palette of some crazed abstract artist

Obsessed by the juxtaposition of opposites:
The piercing stab of pink like a surge of joy;
And the dank, grey, concrete pavements of Istanbul.
All day this flower-seller must sit

Measuring the day by the progress
Of cold through bones.
When I buy anenomes, red and blue,
His face flowers into a smile,

His yellow teeth the petals of his own rose.
When I place coins in his hands,
His eyes gleam, sparkling like daisies,
White in a green field under a warm, blue sky.

Istiklal Caddesi

When sunlight falls, it is
The icing on the Istiklal Caddesi,
As buildings shine the intricacy
Of stone carvings into day.

The shout of street sellers
With pens and worry beads
Turns sun into sound,
As street children smile

The mumbo-jumbo of their accordions.
A girl's black hair and dark eyes
Shimmy light along, as she
Dances her gait down the street.

Your muscles relax into their steps.
Trees break up grey stones
With the explosion of moments
Greener than the last.

Bosphorous

A yacht scythes its white sickle
Across the Bosphorous.
A cruiser chisels along,
Creating its white sculpture
Of water and air behind it.
A tug, upright beetle, busies about,
Looking for a tanker.
One turns up,
Impersonating a red cliff
Motoring past us.

Seagulls maraud over the waves,
Looking for hamsi to mug, *
As they glimmer about
Just under the surface.
Sunshine blares out,
Visual ghetto blaster.

A warship lurks,
Quiet armoury of intent.
It treads forward stealthily.
Tiny fishing crafts bob hope about,
Expecting everyone to avoid them.

Sightless, the Bosphorous looks out
And contemplates as cargo boats
Trail Spain, Greece, and others
Past it up to the Black Sea.
Movement moves ceaselessly.
Forward, backward,
Never staying here,
Always going there.

* hamsi (Turkish) = anchovies

Istanbul

Its mosques, domed foreheads
Of Eastern thought,
Frown out from Istanbul's skyline
Like reminders of duty.

Now Istanbul becomes a cormorant
Darning a hole in the water,

Now a fish photoflashing
On the end of a rod and line,

Now a cruiser hotelling past.

Istanbul metamorphoses off,
Becomes Galata Tower,
Swivelling its outlook round
Like an eagle with a revolving neck.
Built to help ships clear out invaders,
This building now soars in peace
Above the mayhem
Of exhausts and horns,
Friend of the sky
And tourists with cameras.

Then Istanbul becomes
A dull-clothed flower seller
Selling the omni-coloured
Flowers of his poverty.

Traffic shoals along
In the silvering sunshine.

Istanbul becomes a mist
In the mind, out of which come
Bright silver brooches,
Multi-decorating the water.

Sometimes Istanbul is itself:
A dark-skinned child with worn shoes
Clinging to her mother;
A military policeman as straight as his rifle;
A grey-haired man in a white linen suit
Strolling with sunglasses and a stick;
Glass towers reflecting the sky;

But most of the time, Istanbul hides
Behind the thoughts I bring.

Metropolis

You are like a motorway
A construction gang works on
But which goes on forever.
When I walk about you,
I see a constant reconstruction
Of the ground under my feet.
You are a redevelopment of the road
Between now and tomorrow,
Though your tunnels and bridges
Seem a labyrinth leading nowhere.

Your people shuffle places incessantly,
And cars and buses blur
One indiscriminate moment into the next.
Your buildings are the higgledy-piggledy of lego
Assembled by some tantrum-led toddler.

There are moments
When I see clearly the yes
In that blue sky you push those high rises into,
But dare I look down
To see what the fall might be?

Toothache (Cappadocia)

Göreme's hills are volcanic lava
Formed by rain into shapes so weird
That I can only describe them
In terms of what they are not:

Shaggy ink-caps;
Upside-down ice-cream cones
Some magician's child fashioned
From his stardust playdough set;

Conical wizards' hats.
And look at that phallus with mouth and eyes,
And a brow furrowed into pigeon lofts.
Its face chipped into real rooms

With shelves and beds hewn out of the rock,
It makes an economical use of landscape.
They filmed *Star Wars* here,
Thinking this the most other-worldly terrain

They could find.
And we wander about Göreme,
Looking for postcards and chocolate,
Try to rescue mundanity from the fabulous.

It's easier to describe us, mankind –
As a form of geometric caries.
Whatever giant these yellow canine teeth belong to
Will one day have us drilled out.

Underground City, Derinkuyu, Cappadocia

A surprise package containing
Blacks and dim yellows, greys and whites,
And wrapped up with
The feel of stone, cold but dry,
And the need to bend low under tunnels
That barked early morning
Bending and stretching exercises at me.

I questioned my way into the earth,
Feeling air cool and sharp,
Fresh from the straight line
Of the ventilation shaft.

A guide lumbered his deep voice
Through his Turkish English,
Piecing together his meanings
By forcing bits of language together,
Like parts of a jigsaw
That weren't made to fit.

Bewildered and blinking
Against the sudden blitz of an artificial light
Lying in ambush round a corner,
I found the underground city all around me,
Like something that had always been there
But which I had never been aware of.

Life chiselled its way into these rocks,
Made its lair dark and safe,
Until it could burst singing into the day
Once the battles were over.

Here a schoolteacher taught a class,
A winemaker trod grapes, a cook cooked.
A family quarrelled and slept,
Stones rolled across tunnels
To protect these people from invaders,
And traps lurked unseen in the darkness.

I felt a kinship with this people,
As if I too have deeper parts
Where I hide when hurt
Till the wars of living depart again.

Ihlara Canyon, Cappadocia

This canyon, its rocks red in the sun,
Was cut out of the volcanic tuff.

We tramped along it, snake-file,
Towards the Church of the Snake.
With a cross-shape hewn into the rock,

It had another wall trussed in a serpent body
That writhed along it in green –
Only reborn in the dark womb of the cave
By the flicker of our hand-held torches.

Then we were out in the sunlight,
Peering up at a monastery
Made of holes in a rock face
With two crosses beside them for eyes
Squinnying down on us
As we stumbled past a cave-city.

We trod gingerly over askew stepping-stones,
Then bent backs under overhanging rocks
Towards the end of our journey:

Two donkeys with four brown-skinned children,
Who asked us for torches or hats;
And our mini-bus gleaming in sunlight
Like a misplaced harbour-light,
And ready to whisk us away, wondering,
Back to the rain of Istanbul
And the queuing in concrete supermarkets
For water and ekmek. *

* ekmek (Turkish) = bread

Building Block (High School – Istanbul)

They dug a hole in the playground
Big enough to hold the principal
And all the vice-principals,
But they didn't put them in it.

They did rip the walls
Out of most of the classes,
Hired a frantic drilling machine
To drown out the sound
Of any teacher left teaching,
And compressed the students
Into the rooms that were left.

Some students liked it.
They couldn't get any work done.
Others objected that 'cramming'
Was never meant to be like this.

We continued droning on about
English Literature and phrasal verbs,
In the hope that someone might be
Mortaring together a more plausible future.

Afternoon Off

This school has released its gladness
Hurrying a ball along,
Passing liberty about,
Racing lightness.

They cartwheel joy on grass before stopping
To stretch arms for the proferred
Orange of soft drinks,
The hard, cracking crust of biscuits,
And lie back chatting the afternoon.

The grey of their uniforms is a lie here.
Life is the blueness of a pond,
The brightness of sunlight
On glass in the café window.

We are in the park,
Fingering creeping shadows on benches,
Learning the lessons of late afternoon sunlight,
That the now of warmth and greenness
Fades quickly.

For a moment,
We forget the confines
Of classrooms and courses,
Feed our lungs,
Touch the world
With our trembling fingers.

Suicide

She became words whispered in corners in dread,
An untidy arrangement of skin and bone
On the pavement underneath the window
That she jumped from;
A hymn at assembly quavered in the courtyard
In the autumn breeze;
An empty desk no one dared sit in – at first;
A paragraph in a paper under an advert for catfood.

She exchanged warmth, touch, smell
For a moment's unwelcome memory
Among football, exams, rock music, boy friends.

Her life passed from window to ground
In a scream at the world:
'I won't take part in your system, your digital lives'.

She sought to impose her ideas on our lack of them
In the letter she wrote to us.
To make us improve our world,
As we watched our contentment on our TVs
And played at intergalactic war
In the space cruisers on our computers.

The Disquiet

Hair dishevelled by a morning's fingers pondering,
Gait a shambling weariness,
She suffers along the corridor between classes.
Her thoughts shuffling just ahead of her,

Kicking at the next class,
The point she forgot to make in the last,
The student who spoke out of turn.
She jerks out greetings in the staffroom,

Reaches herself into a seat at a desk,
Mutters over marking,
Declines through the verb 'to be'
Into more weariness,

Ticks the wrong spelling of 'it's',
Scores out the right one
In her mind, before organising herself
Into the correct answer. And yet...

Through this needling pain,
She becomes aware that
Nothing has yet gone seriously wrong –
Though there is next week's

Play / magazine / concert to come.
Sunlight makes a surprise assault on her irritability,
Slashing through the window.
She looks out to the street

With its moving out and beyond
Of cars angling off.
Her mind sheers away
Like a cliff lunging

When she thinks of anything bar
Marking, preparation, teaching.
She avoids the idea of hope
Greening out in the park beyond,

Of distance reaching out like a promise.
She can't think past the rebelliousness of youth,
Their angry responses,
The familiarity of this comforting disquiet.

Mothering

So this is what that sea of yowling
That drowned my night
Trickled away to:

This three-inch squeal for a mother;
A ginger-and-white fur-roll
Squirming helplessness and hunger.

Now the mother's shrill chirrup
Stretches out her teated tortoiseshellness.
The companionship of milk is warm,

A flick of a clawless paw,
A lick of a pliant tongue,
The kittens' fierce toothy hug at full paps,

Leaving me out of it,
The person who puts down the bowl
Of chicken, the saucer of water.

Looking Through Yesterday's Trouser Pockets

I found something moving in the trouser leg,
That was not the trouser leg I was moving.

In the dark, a nonsense world
Was waving about,

Whiskers touched walls that glided,
Claws tore at outer space.

I delved open the trousers, brought the room in
That the kitten remembered.

Kayser was white, ginger, long-haired,
Blue-eyed, tiny, ready to pounce claws at me

For bringing back the sky from wherever it had gone.
I put the kitten in the chair

Fond familiar of what the right way up is,
Kayser semtexed a paw at me. I purred.

Hilal (The Fever After The Operation)

She gazed at a checked blanket
As if afraid it might disappear.

She was well dug into her space
But had already been outflanked by her bandaged paw

And the fur shaved off on her side after the operation.
Quietness crept round the room,

Ashamed not to be chirruping
And rubbing hunger round your legs

As you opened the fridge door.
There, catfood piled precariously on top of itself

To become mountains of regret
While we kept buying more to tempt her.

But her yearning only burned bright
In the calm turbulence of her defence

Of that hollowed out blanket
Occupied by the forceless force of her thinning body.

Hilal (Recovering)

She looks surprised
At the easy way
She breathes,
At the sunlight
She feels on her fur.

She ricochets a glance
Round the room,
Sees the fridge,
A cup of water
Beside it.

Some pale chicken
On a dark brown plate
Reminds her of
What hunger is.

Walking towards it
Is an adventure
In balance,
A memory of movement,
Done by rote
Without understanding.

She is a tortoiseshell,
Look of apprehension
At her lack of pain,
At the new interest
She has in things
Past her checked blanket.

Suddenly she gawks
Pleasure at me

As if it were easy.

Here Again

In the bahçe, the arm *
Of a bamboo chair frames a sea,
The Bosphorous, as it squirms through Istanbul.
Cooling umbrellas flap shade slowly.

I am tucked inside the heat
Like something slipped firmly into a packet.
No room for moving.

I look out to a cargo boat
Trailing shredded water behind it,
Black, its twin cranes
Standing firm in their opposite directions.

Trees step up the slope on the opposite shore
From apartment block to apartment block,
Till they have frogmarched a hill into a landscape.

I remember we shared this,
As the light hopscotched over the water,
The lift of the breeze for a moment
Like a quickening of the pulse

So that whenever I look over this scene,
You are here again.

* bahçe (Turkish) = tea-garden

Coming Out On The Plane Soon

Haar thick as a dry-stone dyke,
Fog-stone upon fog-stone
Across the Bosphorous,
Separating Europe and Asia
With a wall of wisps
Till morning sunlight
Cracked it here and there.

Asia peeked across,
Slowly lifting this rock
As if it were a curtain.

Out there was a fleet
Of small fishing boats
Lifting lines into fish.
They clarified the mist
Into their own shapes.

A white boat edged
Forward, pushed by
Its put-put of sound.

A man peered across
The wheel into light
Growing stronger.
I saw behind him
The trees and houses
That had been
Forbidden existence.

Light tumbled over the water,
A troop of acrobats
Putting on a show
On the up and down
Of the waves.

I watched them,
Glad the fog had gone,
Thinking of you,
Coming out on the plane soon.

Now That You've Gone Away Again

I keep bumping into the places
Where you were.
I didn't notice before
That your slight figure
Filled every room.

I squeeze into them,
Hugging the walls
And trying to avoid you,
But the space you possessed is everywhere.

The chair you laughed in still chuckles.
The book you touched
Still has the warmth
Of your hand on it.
Your breath kneads mine.

I open all the windows
To let the air and light rush in,
But there you are, not striding
Up the road to the shop
In your navy-blue linen shirt
And cotton Calvin Kleins,
With the wind in your auburn hair,
And wearing that smile about something
I never understood,
Gracing the very street
With the presence of your absence.

New Horizons, Antalya

Empty the mind of Istanbul.
Fill it with rocks, caves, sea, and sky.

There is no limit to thought
But the world it knows.

Here, mountains push up
On the shoulders of others.

Light abseils down the sky.
A boat motors out from here

To the million theres
I cannot yet conceive of.

Odd Angle, Antalya

The tractor was grinding the boat
Level again, levering at it

With noise and steadiness.
Broken-angled under the water,

It was a parody of boatness
And nothing to be done about it

Except gradually,
A long moment renewing itself

Until the boat was healed.
At the end of my school-term

I was aslant to the world,
Odd-tempered, unnerved,

Not feeling as solid as a boat
Till I looked at this one.

I hoped this holiday
In Antalya would straighten

Me up to the horizontal angle
That calm waters have.

The View From The Restaurant, Antalya

Mountains tear a jagged strip
Of blackness out of the sky.
Lights are on the move again,
Panthering along that road above the sea,

Stalking the beam ahead.
The sky continues its process
Of compressing its reds, oranges, and purples
Into such a small space they disappear.

A small boat leads the ruly rhythm
Of its engine across the bay
Where the wind folds over the waves.
And darkness piles itself upon itself

Till it is as big as the sky.
We look out, sip wine,
Mouth grilled chicken,
Touch light fingers.

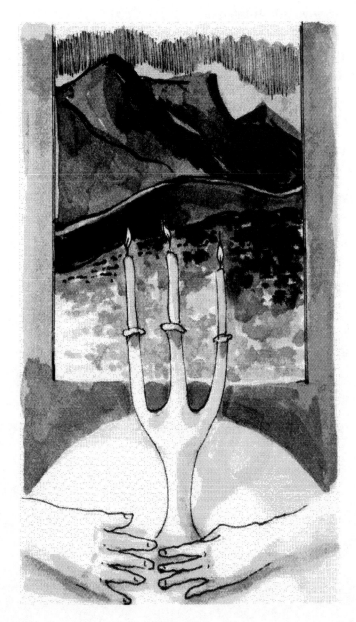

Free-wheel, Antalya

This sight-echo that the waves do,
Repeating 'sun' all day long, lulls us.

Stretched loose on this sunbed
On the deck of this boat

That frees this moment from the last
And gives us this coast along,

We watch cliffs revving past,
Caves burrowing their way out,

Slip our way to Duden Waterfall,
Where the rainbow landscapes it.

We are tourists who photograph everything,
We try to trap time in our boxes

So that we can put Duden waterfall
In a cupboard at home and forget

To regret it, while we hurry along
In our cars and buses

Beneath the multi-storey skyscrapers
That touch nothing but the earth.

Cat-Time, Antalya

Black-and-white
Fur-stroke of warmth,
Purr-space of time,

My knee cats
Through the morning
Peaceful and slow

While the sun
Clothes my neck
With warm silk

And a cool breeze
Touches me gently,
As if with wonder.

By these Roman walls,
A harbour laps light,
Boats creak, yawn,
Mountains stretch repose
Out to the horizon.

A cat has pounced
This quietness at me,

Licks my hand
Free of cares,

Curls time round
In a tight ball

And keeps it safe.

Rainy Day, Antalya

This drizzle has all day
To weather at our hopes
Of sunshine in Antalya,
With its persistent rhythming down of rain;
Its funeral march through the day.

Those tumble-down clouds
Seem as rickety as some of these roofs,
Ready to collapse under all that grey.
A palm tree, tall, as lean as an athlete,
Droops its hung-over leaves.

It is quiet. No one else
Shelters in this outdoor café
With its rain-raddled thatch
And its view of minarets
And modern apartment blocks.

The day drips
Its steady drizzle of minutes
Counting out our stay.

Amphitheatre, Ephesus

I

Broken grey wire sentries
The green and brown scrub badly
But imprisons time.

We walk to meet St Paul at the amphitheatre,
Marvel at the publicness of the public latrine,
Borrow the Library of Celsus for an afternoon.

We ogle along the Sacred Way,
Linger our looks passionately at an Ionic column,
Caress a broken arch,

As we wonder at the tumble-down of time
And the pick-me-up of nostalgia.
And what prayers led to this anyway?

Perhaps the same prayers in the shops
That lay along these roads,
As there are in those that trade today

On the road that leads to the entrance,
Where they shock their silver jewellery
And ceramic blue tiles at the sun

On the Way of Postcards and Maps,
Where the Turks stand around
Praying for tourists.

II

An amphitheatre,
Seats shouldering each other

Up to the sky.
Gladiators flexed murder

Round the staging.
Chasseed a cunning slash,

Shimmied trained muscles to
The point of balance of life or death

Never a glance at the gorging stares
Of the spectators

Semi-circling these executions
With applause.

Their eternal mortality
Of the gladiators

Writhes now on this page
For you, also their spectators,

Curious at the otherness
Of the common fate, death.

III

And St Paul preached here.
That Dutch bible-belter
With the enraptured smile
Will tell you

Of Paul's fierce dialogue
With a tiered audience
Piling rage upon rage
Fierce as beasts in rut

As in the camel fighting in modern Selcuk,
A quick paw of words,
A heave with a sentence,
The prolonged shoving of a verbiose paragraph

As the ideas fought out their gladiatorial rage.
The guidebook tells you that
They put Paul in a prison on a hill,
Though this modern evangelical Christian

Claims ancient respect for free speech.
The miracle is that history is what
We want it to be, isn't it
Here in the theatre of time?

IV

If I see another headless statue
I think I'll scream.

Someone must have had fun
Knocking off all these crania.

In Egypt, Christians defaced Egyptian gods;
In Ephesus, the private parts of past Emperors

Have been pummelled.
New cultures must destroy old

Or so it seems.

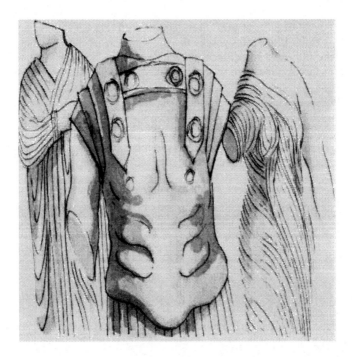

V

A bird sidles up to tourists
As they fritter their crumbs,
Has a stab at life then away,
Its day a series of sorties.

It's a dull brown person of a bird to look at –
With green soup spilled down its front –
Who performs guerrilla operations
On the rotating leavings of tourists.

There is no fight to be won with glory here,
Just the slow attrition of the bird's
Tempered beak on our morsels,
The slow, careful wearing-down at hunger.

VI

Turks too hunt you down,
Approach with netting smiles

The spear of their sales talk ready.
They wait on the road for tourists,

Offer taxis, coins, guide work.
They will not take no very easily.

Just what's in your wallet.
The gladiatorial test is still here,

Dallying amongst these hills
In the blood of the evening sun.

You hadn't expected
These desperate minutes.

But they were always here,
Waiting for you.

VII

Time presses its boot upon me,
Walks on and through me.
My moment passes.

My blood spills.
The poem is done.
Here in the amphitheatre

With the cold stone
And the hot-blooded memories,
The words fought back.

They won.
They wrote
What they needed to.

Postcards

Memories are postcards
Sent by myself to myself:

A picture of Cape Wrath,
The lighthouse overseeing Sandwood Bay
With its stack daggering at the sky,
Guillemots head-butting their way
Through the waves after the fish,
Puffins spattering the cliffs
With the colour of their fluorescent busyness –
Wish you were here;

A photograph of Balnakeil Beach,
Dunes tall, curved like biceps,
Flexing the silence of marram grass
By the shadows where I waded,
Feet questing into the softness of sand –
Wish I was there.

These postcards are sent
To tell me there is a here, a now
In Balnakeil.

Not everywhere is Istanbul,
Winter's cough erupting in my chest,
Traffic howling at me,
The bony push of the market,
The acrid smell of the Bosphorous'
Milky wastes.

Somewhere, there is a wind
Blowing in the tang of the Atlantic
As gulls lift like hope.

Return

I have come back to see
This view of Balnakeil House
Standing up to the bay,
Sand, sea, and sky,
Exploding in the brain
Like an hallucination.

Clover flowers fist
Their white out of the grass;
Pansy tongues lap violet;
Bird's Foot Trefoils
Step out yellow
Over the moor.

I loose my legs off
Towards the horizon,
Muscles pushing,
Grass yielding its spring
Past the 'klee klee' of some bird
I do not know.

Hills clamber over each other,
Try to outclimb the sky.
The clouds ravel themselves.
Sand dunes hunch against the weather.
The breeze air-brushes
My skin, cooling.

I reach a cliff imploding
With puffins and holes,
Watch one bird
Unleash flight
In a tornado of wings.
Then I stride out again.

This is Durness.
After minarets and kebabs,
This push up of a Scottish Primrose,
Its stalked eye
Goggling purple
At the sight of me

Highland Loch

I slick the line on to the water. The boat
Creaks the rhythm of the Atlantic wind

As it skims waves down the loch.
The cuff of my green oilskin rubs

The flick of my wrist into my own skin.
I push the flies through the air over and over,

As if they form part of some trying gym machine.
A fish tugs petulance at a fly, as if

Annoyed by an insult. I do not hook him.
The weather girns on. Rain stutters

Its wetness against my cheek, then away –
But it will return. These clouds say so

With their dark swirling. I push my muscles
And rod down the loch. I will kill a fish or I will not

But this repetition of sinew will
Find itself caught in my memory.

Cattle On Balnakeil Beach

Darker than angry thoughts,
These black cattle, swaying amiability

With their tails, hips, and jaws,
As they chew over the end of the day.

The sun lowers itself gingerly into the sea,
As if testing the temperature, which is now cool.

Over and through sand,
Their hooves dig in and kick back.

There is an ominous peacefulness
In these twenty or so cattle looming in the half-dark;

They are walking bulks armed with their size.
I had meant to walk here but skirt round,

Give way to the might of a bovine stroll.

Café Moments, Stromness (Weekend Visit)

1

The blue stretched fabric
That covers the sky
Looks a bit worn
Just above the mountains.

2

Rain.
Yet another coffee cup.
The sound of fork on plate.
Rain
Hanging by raintips
On to window glass,
Each minute hung on to the next
By rain.
Voices reverberate lassitude
Round the café.
The rain monotones on.

3

The evening gleam
Of wine glass and polished table
Puts a gloss on our stay.
Waitresses pitter-patter
Plates round the room.
Stromness unwinds itself
Into a bottle of wine.
Candles gutter light.
A holiday day
Reaches its full conclusion,
As a morsel of fish
Flakes the sea's swell and ebb
On to my tongue.
Our eyes talk.

Ruckus, Balnakeil, Sutherland

These cliffs are outcrops of sanity
Amidst some jetting racket,
As low-flying planes
Draw their ruckus
So close past each other that
They seem to interweave flight paths.

People never leave this landscape alone.
Tourists spatter higgledy-piggledy
Footprints across the beach.
Sailboards outburst yellow.
Sea-going vessels define
Horizons past us.

But the hills, sea, and sand
Ignore all this.
The grass on those dunes
Is a pool swirling the mind
With its greenness,
As the bay laps up another century.

ABOUT THE AUTHOR

James Andrew was born in Aberdeen in 1952. This is his second published collection of poems. He has also had many poems published in magazines.

He is a teacher, presently working in Turkey, which is where most of these poems are set. A few others are set in his home of Durness, in Scotland.

The poems express his reaction to the Turkish culture; they also express the contrast between city and country life.

Istanbul, his base in Turkey, has a population of about fifteen million. Durness, where he lives in Scotland, has a population of about 350.

In the summer, he often helps his wife in her craft shop in Balnakeil Craft Village in Durness.

James Andrew has an M. Litt in Creative Writing from St. Andrews University.

ABOUT THE ILLUSTRATOR

Ishbel Macdonald, DA, studied painting at Glasgow School of Art. After a post-graduate year with a four-month travelling scholarship spent in Spain, she eventually settled in Northwest Sutherland.

She began to work in the medium of print and opened The Printmakers' Gallery in Balnakeil Craft Village in 1988, where she still exhibits.

Her work is in private collections all over the world and has also been acquired by BBC Scotland, The Scottish Executive, and Inverness District Council.

The illustrations for this book were completed after visiting Istanbul itself.

Most of what she produces is based on the landscape where she lives in Sutherland, but she has recently held an exhibition of her paintings of Iceland, another of her favourite destinations.

Her gallery is sought out by tourists every year on their return to Northwest Sutherland.